George Frideric Handel

GREAT
ORGAN CONCERTI
Opp. 4 and 7
in Full Score

George Frideric Handel

GREAT ORGAN CONCERTI
Opp. 4 and 7
in Full Score

From the Deutsche Händelgesellschaft Edition
Edited By
Friedrich Chrysander

Dover Publications, Inc., New York

Published in Canada by General Publishing Company, Ltd., 30 Lesmill Road, Don Mills, Toronto, Ontario.
Published in the United Kingdom by Constable and Company, Ltd.

This Dover edition, first published in 1983, is an unabridged republication of all 12 Organ Concerti from Volume 28 of *Georg Friedrich Händel's Werke* as originally published by the Deutsche Händelgesellschaft in Leipzig in 1868.

The publisher is grateful to the Sibley Music Library of the Eastman School of Music, Rochester, N.Y., for making its material available for reproduction.

Manufactured in the United States of America
Dover Publications, Inc., 180 Varick Street, New York, N.Y. 10014

Library of Congress Cataloging in Publication Data

Handel, George Frideric, 1685–1759.
  [Concertos, organ, orchestra]
  Twelve organ concerti from the Deutsche Händelgesellschaft Edition.

  Originally published in 1738 (op. 4) and 1760 (op. 7)
  Contents: Op. 4. No. 1, in G minor/G major. No. 2, in B-flat major. No. 3, in G minor. No. 4, in F major. No. 5, in F major. No. 6, in B-flat major—Op. 7. No. 1, in B-flat major. No. 2, in A major. No. 3, in B-flat major. No. 4, in D minor. No. 5, in G minor. No. 6, in B-flat major.
  1. Concertos (Organ) I. Chrysander, Friedrich, 1826–1901.
M1005.H13C62 1983   82-17769
ISBN 0-486-24462-8

Contents

Opus 4 (originally published in London, 1738)
    No. 1, in G Minor/Major   1
    No. 2, in B-flat Major   20
    No. 3, in G Minor   31
    No. 4, in F Major   41
    No. 5, in F Major   56
    No. 6, in B-flat Major   61

Opus 7 (originally published in London, 1761)
    No. 1, in B-flat Major   68
    No. 2, in A Major   85
    No. 3, in B-flat Major   97
    No. 4, in D Minor   110
    No. 5, in G Minor   121
    No. 6, in B-flat Major   130

The Opus 4 concerti are sometimes referred to as Handel's organ concerti nos. 1–6; the Opus 7 concerti, as nos. 7–12. Of the two minuets in Op. 7, no. 3, the first (A; p. 108) was the original one, bearing in the MS the date the whole composition was ended (January 4, 1757); whereas the second (B; p. 109) occurs on a supplementary MS sheet without the organ part, which is supplied (in smaller notation) from the first printed edition.

Opus 4, No. 1, in G Minor/Major

Opus 4, No. 2, in B-flat Major

Opus 4, No. 3, in G Minor

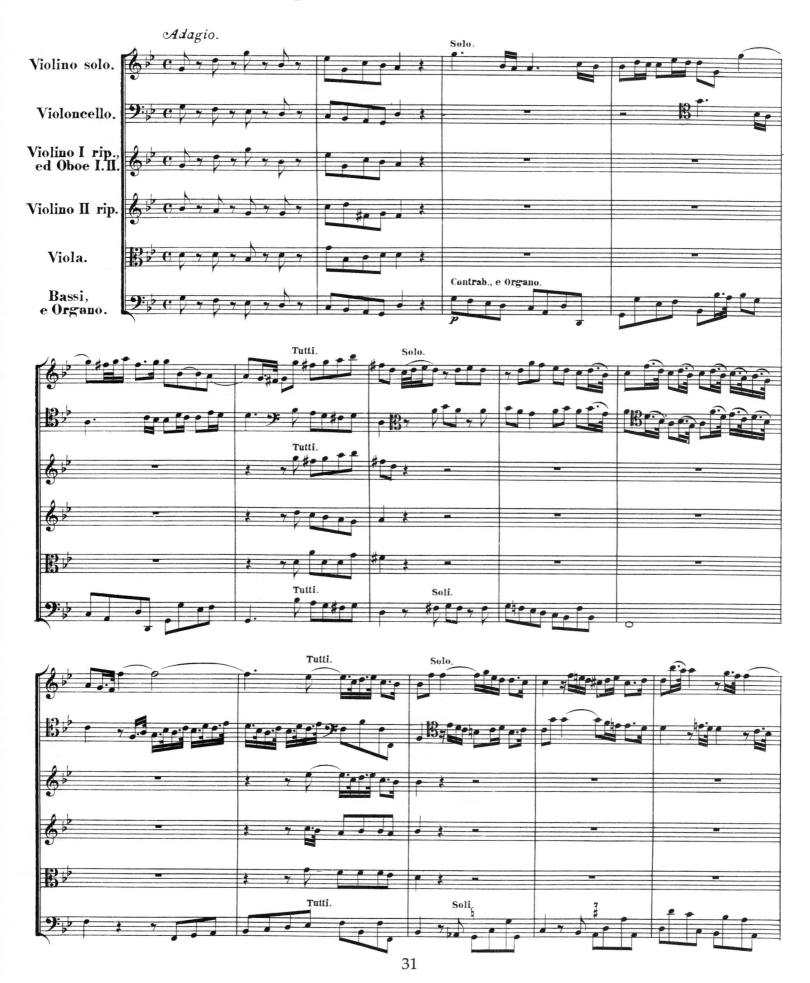

Opus 4, No. 4, in F Major

Opus 4, No. 5, in F Major

Opus 4, No. 6, in B-flat Major

61

Larghetto.

Viol. s. Flauti.

Viol. s. Flauti.

64   Opus 4, No. 6

Allegro moderato.

Opus 7, No. 1, in B-flat Major

Organo a 2 Clav. e Pedale.
un poco piano.

BOURRÉE.

Opus 7, No. 2, in A Major

OUVERTURE.

85

✻) Statt des folgenden halben Taktes steht
im Original diese längere Ausführung
für Organo solo.

✻) *Instead of the next half-bar the original*
MS. has the following longer passage
for Organo solo.

Organo
ad libitum.

Opus 7, No. 3, in B-flat Major

A. Menuet.

B. MENUET.

Violino I.II.
Oboe I.II.

Violino III,
e Viola.

Organo.

Bassi.

Opus 7, No. 4, in D Minor

Violino I.
Oboe I.

Violino II.
Oboe II.

Viola.

Organo.

Bassi.

Allegro.

Tutti.

Solo.

*Organo
ad libitum.*

Opus 7, No. 5, in G Minor

Opus 7, No. 6, in B-flat Major

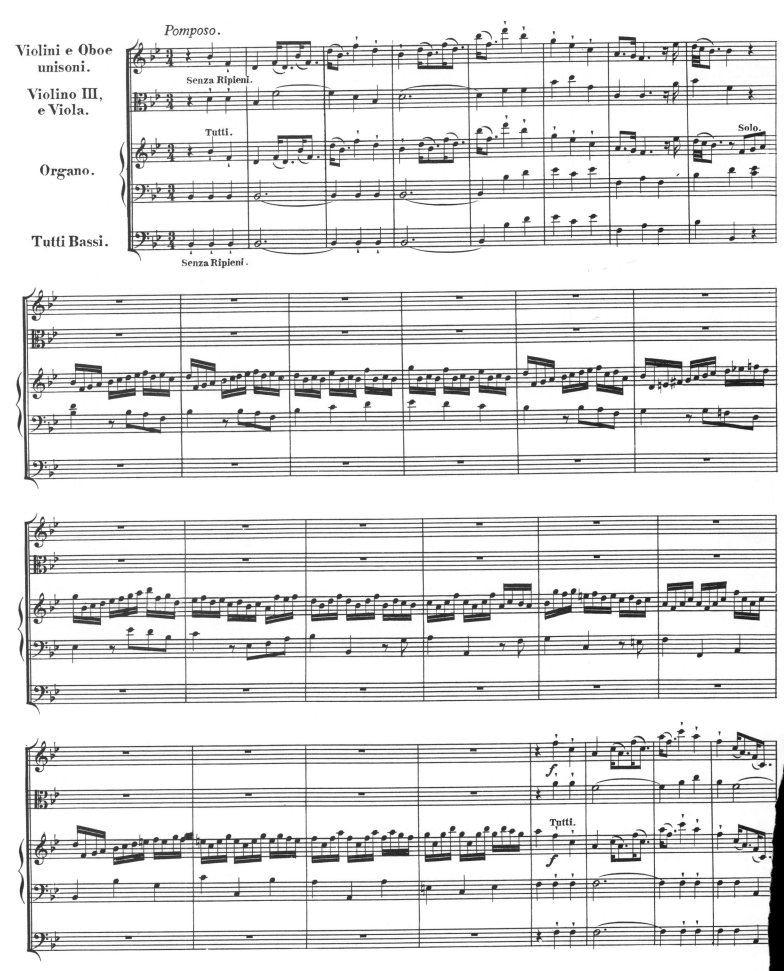

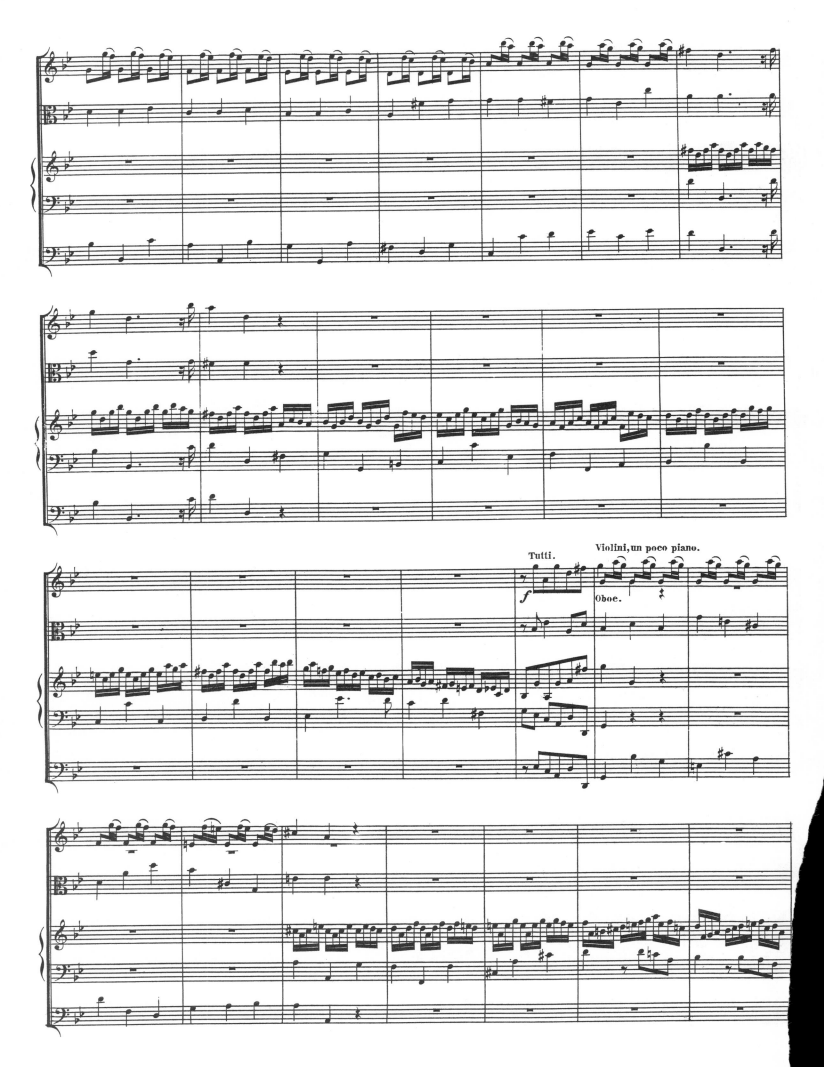